ISABELLA BREGA

Washington

PRIDE AND GLORY OF AMERICA

SMITHMARK

WASHINGTON

CONTENTS

Text
Isabella Brega

Graphic design
Patrizia Balocco
Alberto Bertolazzi

Editorial coordination
Viviana Valmacco
Alberto Bertolazzi

Translation
Jane Glover

This edition published in 1997 by Smithmark Publishers, a division of U.S. Media Holdings, Inc., 16 East 32nd Street, New York, NY 10016.

SMITHMARK books are available for bulk purchase, for sales promotion and premium use. For details write or call the manager of special sales, SMITHMARK Publishers, 16 East 32nd Street, New York, NY 10016; (212) 532-6600.

Produced by: White Star S.r.l. Via Candido Sassone, 22/24 13100 Vercelli, Italy.

ISBN: 0-76519401-5

Printed in February 1997 by Tien Wah Press, Singapore

1 The Capitol is the seat of the federal American Congress, the organ of legislative power comprising the Senate and House of Representatives, and is one of the most representative buildings of the American capital.

2-3 A panoramic shot showing the Mall, the long, straight avenue surrounded by green lawns which ideally links the seat of executive power, the White House, with that of legislative power, the Capitol building.

4-5 The Thomas Jefferson Memorial is an imposing monument built in the classical style, standing on the southern side of the small lake known as the Tidal Basin.

6-7 The Lincoln Memorial, one of the most famous monuments in the United States, rises in line with the Capitol building at the western end of the Mall, in West Potomak Park. It was built in 1922 to a design by Henry Bacon, in the shape of a Grecian temple.

8 The building housing the National Archives was built in 1935 to a classical design by John Russell Pope, one of the architects who contributed to creating the face of the American capital. He was also the creator of the National Gallery and the Jefferson Memorial.

9 The Capitol's huge white cupola, topped with the bronze statue of Liberty, takes its inspiration from the Basilica of St. Peter in Rome and St. Paul's Cathedral in London, England.

10-11 The Thomas Jefferson Building is the main building of the Library of Congress, which was founded in 1800. The building is in the Italian Renaissance style and dates from 1886-1897. The library, which was initially reserved for members of Congress is now open for reference use and houses 36 million manuscripts and 27 million books, including the 6,487 volumes of Thomas Jefferson's private library.

INTRODUCTION

Washington: glory, pride and remembrance. Capital and history of a nation state and world power. For the more than 18 million tourists who come here every year, the enduring role of the American metropolis is to be the emblem of a superpower. More than a city, Washington is a monument which America has erected to itself and to its own role.

For a citizen of the United States, to travel to Washington is not merely to undertake a journey, it is to go on pilgrimage, to those places which residents only notice when they have guests with them.

The souvenir photograph in front of the Capitol building, the guided tour of the White House, the dash to the National Air and Space Museum, the stroll down the long lawns of the

Mall, which links the seat of Congress to the Lincoln Memorial, the jog along the C&O Canal. Even though residents have been rendered almost immune to this wealth of monuments through living in daily contact with them, Washington was intentionally created to be the most scenically grandiose town in the United States.

The layout, the open spaces, the proportions, everything was designed to arouse awe, by the French architect Pierre L'Enfant, in 1791. The Lincoln Memorial was devised to be viewed humbly, visitors gradually approaching on foot, until when they reach their destination they are almost crushed by the seated statue of the sixteenth president of the United States, who towers from a height of more than nine metres. But it is not just the great number of national museums filled with works by the world's most important artists or the abundance, in contrast to their relative scarcity in the rest of the country, of picture-postcard monuments, which make every American believe it to be their sacred duty to visit their capital city. This is where the public and private spheres meet and intertwine, before separating once again, but not before they have attained a new awareness and motivation. For the citizens of the United States, who live scattered over an enormous territory, being

12-13 The 169-metre-high Washington Memorial is dedicated to the first American president. Started in 1848 to plans by Robert Mills, but only completed in 1884, it was supposed to be sited on the same axis as the Capitol building, but the ground chosen for its location was subject to subsidence and it was moved about a hundred metres out of line with the Mall.
In 1855, due to the theft by the anticlerical group called the Know-Nothings of a block of marble donated by Pope Pius IX from the Temple of Concord in Rome, (the block was probably thrown into the Potomac), work was suspended and only started again in 1876. Considered one of the principal symbols of the American capital city, the obelisk dedicated to George Washington was to have had a circular base like a Greek temple, but it was never built. Today the monument is surrounded by the fifty flags of the American states.

14 top The building which houses the United States Supreme Court, the highest organ of judicial power, is in white Vermont marble and was built in 1935 to a design by Cass Gilbert, its shape inspired by the architecture of a Grecian temple, while its outer facade is in the neo-classical style.

14 bottom The impressive monumental stance of the Thomas Jefferson Memorial is underlined on the Mall side by the stretch of water known as the Tidal Basin, which mirrors the building and magnifies its scenic power.

15 The photograph shows a detail of the Arlington Memorial Bridge, one of many which span the Potomac, built during the years 1926-1932 to a design by McKim, Mead and White. The bridge, which lies behind the Lincoln Memorial, at the western end of the Mall, forms a conceptual link between the monument dedicated to the fourth president of the United States and the Arlington National Cemetery in Virginia where John F. Kennedy, assassinated in 1963, is buried amongst officers and enlisted men.

able to say "I was there" is to grasp what this citizenship means. It is the chance not only to see, but to "become part" of history, to give their own lives a national dimension. Yesterday, today, tomorrow: arrival point of a historical process, subject of the present, promise for the future. Like all capital cities, Washington belongs not to itself but to the world. It is a point of reference not just for a nation, but for a civilisation which, for better and for worse, continues to look to the United States as a model for development and for freedom. A city of palaces, statues and museums, all designed to emphasise its role, it is also a place of gardens and lakes which lighten the historical grandeur crystallised in the crushing size of its monumentality — power frozen in the ataraxy of icy, white, polished marble. To be and to become: trees, flowers and ponds, all breathing life into and tempering the rigid pomp of this city-capital which is very much a capital, infinitely reflecting and multiplying the image of a metropolis of a thousand cultures. Henry Kissinger, ex-Secretary of State, used to say that whenever a revolution breaks out in some country, they open another ethnic restaurant in Washington, and it is true that, in addition to the already enormous concentration of foreigners, embassies, legations, journalists and international bodies, since the 1960s the city has no longer been the exclusive property of the WASPs (the establishment consisting of White Anglo-Saxon Protestants), but has become a real ethnic mixture. It has the greatest number of Indian, Malaysian, Afghan and Pakistani restaurants in any American city; it has places of worship for all creeds: the neo-Gothic Washington Cathedral, the Romanesque-Byzantine architecture of the Roman Catholic National Shrine of the Immaculate Conception, the turreted Mormon temple, the Islamic Center's mosque, the Washington Hebrew Congregation synagogue; the Adams Morgan area is home to communities of every race and colour.

Washington, the pride. Bureaucratic capital, ministerial empire, kingdom of the clerical class: it was natural that the city should look to the triumphant monumentality of classical

architecture for its inspiration, clothing the forms of its power with marbles and tympana. This Virginian city, which manages to be simultaneously a homage to the great European civilisations and the prototype of the new style of a new world where the American myth lives on, still projects an image of America as unique, original and different.
But like all giants, Washington too has feet of clay.
Despite the presence of the granitic totems of America's enormous power in the world — the FBI, the CIA and the Pentagon — it has to reckon with a daily reality which is not always one of greatness, but one of scandals, corruption, cynicism and delinquency — and racial tension.
But then, the white marble city of the Capitol and the White House is really a black city, run by a black mayor and three quarters of whose inhabitants are black. An area like Old Anacostia is a match for Harlem and one in four inhabitants lives below the poverty line.
The capital, whose record of violent crime competes with Chicago's — it has the third highest number of murders in America — is currently going through a crisis: the middle class is fleeing to the suburbs and from a population of 800,000 in the 1950s, the number has fallen to less than 600,000 today. Washington, the memory. The metropolis, pride and historical conscience of the United States, knows neither regrets nor sadness, but has the courage not to ignore the guilt.
Here there are monuments to the glory and the monument to the mud: the great white bubble of the Capitol which unites the destinies of the Americans, the black granite wall of those who fell in Vietnam, lacerated by the names of the almost 60,000 dead, which divides them. The United States, with the oldest system of government amongst the major Western nations (except for Great Britain) is no longer a young country.
The Civil War and then the Vietnam War marked the loss of its innocence, but on the hill at Arlington, before the flame which burns on the tomb of John F. Kennedy, America, despite everything, still believes.

16 Open all year, day and night, the Lincoln Memorial is a magnet for visitors, drawn by the gigantic statue of Abraham Lincoln. The statue was the creation of the sculptor Daniel Chester French, but the work was actually done by the Italo-American Piccirilli brothers.

17 The outer colonnade of the rotunda of the Thomas Jefferson Memorial, was charged at the time of its construction with imprisoning the big bronze statue by Rudolph Evans. The monument, begun in 1939 and finished in 1943, was designed by John Russell Pope.

18-19 The National Air and Space Museum was inaugurated in 1976 and very soon became one of the world's best-known museum collections. It is part of the Smithsonian Institution, the prestigious institute whose aim is to spread scientific knowledge and it is visited by more than 10 million people a year. Amongst others, its exhibits include the Spirit of St. Louis, the aircraft in which Charles Lindberg crossed the Atlantic in 1927, the 1903 Flyer built by the Wright brothers, an identical missile to the one which launched the first American satellite and even the model of the starship Enterprise which was used for the famous TV series, "Star Trek".

20-21 The crowded Pavillon at the Old Post Office is a modern shopping centre full of cafés, restaurants and shops, housed in the neo-Romantic building dating from 1899. The building is the city's second highest after the Washington Memorial and has a fantastic bell-tower, complete with peel of bells called the Congress Bells which are rung on special occasions. From its top visitors have a splendid view out over the city. The building, located in the group of government buildings built in the 1930s and known as the Federal Triangle, also hosts live shows, which makes it one of the best-known meeting places in the US capital.

A CAPITAL AND
A CITY

Although a capital city by birth, Washington has still had to struggle to become great. Initially, at least, it was so only in its designers' intentions. The largest concentration of monuments anywhere in America, with 40 museums, 150 historic sites and buildings, immense parks and gardens; the magnificent metropolis animated by statues, temples, pantheons, colonnades and majestic palaces; a city of grandiloquence and rhetoric, with its set scenes of imperial prospects and long avenues designed for parades, grew slowly and with difficulty. Officially founded in 1793, until only a few decades ago it was considered a hardship posting for diplomats, to such an extent that at the beginning of the 19th century one French Ambassador was moved to ask himself,

"What have I done to be condemned to live in a city like this?". But then, in 1799, Abigail, wife of President John Adams and the second First Lady, had become lost in the marshes surrounding the Federal City on her way to take up residence there and when, in 1801, Thomas Jefferson was sworn in on Capitol Hill, the Washington which lay around him was only an agglomeration of muddy roads, marshland and modest houses. In 1842, it had nothing to show the English writer Charles Dickens but an empty shell: "Spacious avenues, that begin in nothing and lead nowhere; streets, milelong, that only want houses, roads, and inhabitants; public buildings that need but a public to be complete, and ornaments of great thoroughfares, which only lack great thoroughfares to ornament". Such a disappointment, in fact, that he was led to the conclusion that what they called the City of the Magnificent Distances should really be called the City of the Magnificent Intentions.
The young President of the United States, George Washington, in his letter to the Marquis de Lafayette (April 1783), wrote that the United States, being at last one of the nations of the earth, should build itself an identity.
And in order to create this identity the young American republic had to build itself a capital, drawing widely upon

22-23 Designed by Dr. William Thornton, the Capitol building is set on a hill at the end of the Mall. It was started on 18th September 1793, when George Washington laid the foundation stone. The choice of Thornton's project was not without criticism. For example, in 1806 the architect Benjamin Henry Latrobe commented that the plans for government buildings in Washington were the results of public competitions and the prizes always went to buildings which met with George Washington's approval, but although General Washington was extremely competent in gaining his country's freedom, he knew nothing about art. It should have come as no surprise, Latrobe continued, that the plan by a doctor who knew nothing about architecture should have been chosen for the Capitol building and that by a joiner for the president's house.

24 top The Old Senate
Chamber, which housed the
Senate from 1810 to 1859, still
preserves its original
furnishings.

24-25 Visitors to the Rotunda
inside the Capitol. The large
circular area is decorated
with eight paintings by John
Trumbull and a frieze by
Costantino Brumidi and
Filippo Costaggini
illustrating moments in
American history.

25 top The Statuary Hall
houses a collection of statues
of the most eminent
American citizens, two from
each state.

Greek and Roman history with its wealth of symbols.
Symbols charged with rhetorical meaning, indispensable,
together with the cult of heroes, for a political and cultural
unification, to give a face to the newborn nation.
"Architecture is my deligh" said the third head of state,
Thomas Jefferson, "but it is an enthusiasm of which I am not
ashamed, as its object is to improve the taste of my
countrymen, to increase their reputation, to reconcile them
to the rest of the world, and to procure them its praise".
It was he who had the greatest influence on the city's
development, defining the classical style of the first official
buildings. It is not surprising that in a letter of 1791 Jefferson
was asking William Short to send him a complete series of
Piranesi's designs for the Pantheon, in order to use them for
the public buildings that were to be built.
Roman Pantheons, Egyptian obelisks, Greek temples and
Palladian villas bent to new ends and ideals: all suitable
to dress the present with ancient clothes.
With this casual and pragmatic use (characteristic of the
eclecticism which marked architecture in the United States
from then onwards) of classical forms and referring
principally to the virtues of the Roman Republic, America
sought an ideal and cultural continuation with the Old
World, while at the same time giving expression to its own
independence. Neo-classicism was therefore the right
language to give the young United States a patent of nobility,
to ensure it a respectable pedigree.
The choice of the site for the Federal City appears also to
have been made with reference to the classical era and its
myths. In fact, since the time of Romulus's plough and the
birth of the Eternal City, Rome, that no capital city had come
alive on the basis of such a precise plan and will.
The actual instructions for localising and determining
the square of land on which the city was to rise came from
Washington himself — a signal of the desire to build from
nothing a city which was to be the symbol of a nation born
equal to all others but, at the same time, unlike any of them.
A brand new capital, built on virgin territory, was needed,

26-27 The cupola of the Rotunda in the Capitol building was frescoed by Costantino Brumidi with the Apotheosis of Washington. The cupola is supported by thirty-six columns and the upper lantern rests on a further thirteen, smaller, columns. The numbers correspond respectively to the number of Federal States at the conclusion and the start of work on the building.

in order not to favour any one of the States of the Union; it had to be placed centrally within the nation's territorial boundaries at the time and on a navigable seaway, the Potomac (Powtowmak in the language of the native Americans, meaning river full of fish), which joined it to the Atlantic. Founded on land ceded by the states of Maryland and Virginia, the 100 square miles of the District of Columbia (later reduced to 70), directly administered by the federal government, also included some small towns like Georgetown, Old Anacostia (which became two of the capital's districts) and Alexandria. Hot and humid in the summer, cold in the winter, plagued by marshes and malarial fevers, without any conveniences, Washington was unpopular and almost unpopulated, only totalling 300,000 residents at the beginning of this century.

With its sole importance lying initially in the role it fulfilled, its only task being to govern, until the Second World War it was a capital city with a provincial soul, sleepy and lazy, a city of circulars and ministries: more a capital of bureaucracy than of an empire. It was only in the 1930s, with the enlargement of the clerical class and the creation of the military bureaucratic machine, that it managed to take on an international dimension, reaching a historical peak of 800,000 inhabitants in the 1950s. Today Washington is a vaguely European metropolis which speaks two architectural languages, the classic one of the Mall, its representational centre, and the eclectic one of the rest of the city. As a city it bears witness to the fact that a capital's beauty can derive not so much from the magnificence of its public buildings as from the size of its open spaces and a classical street plan. The layout is centred in the Mall, on two orthogonal intersecting axes centred on the most symbolically significant monuments, and in its rational street plan, in the Jefferson style, rendered less linear by the radial design of its first planner, the French major, Pierre-Charles L'Enfant.

A volunteer in the War of Independence, L'Enfant was a tiresome and difficult man. He received from Washington

27 top left and right The Senate and the House of Representatives took their seats in the building in 1800, seven years after work began. In 1814 the Capitol was destroyed by a fire started by British troops. In 1851-63 the cupola was completed and the north and south wings were added.

the job of giving a face to the new capital and in 1791 presented the plans for the city he intended should be the last of the true Baroque cities. The plan called for imposing buildings for the federal offices, parks and squares within a network of streets intersected diagonally by avenues (the so-called radials) dedicated to the Federal states and a monumental area marked by the avenue of the Mall, running from the Capitol and including the park overlooking the presidential residence, set at right angles to it. It was a grandiose plan, which for economic and political reasons was never fully realised. The architect himself was sacked in 1792 and it was only years later that he received 2,500 of the $90,000 stipulated in the contract.

Several factors intervened in the years which followed to compromise the exact execution of L'Enfant's plan.
The two large rectangular grassed areas of the Mall, at whose intersection an equestrian statue of the first president was supposed to stand, were built, like the avenues which run from the Capitol and the White House, but the equestrian statue was not. It was replaced by an obelisk which was left half-finished for years, due to lack of funds and only finished in 1884. Indeed, the Capitol dome was only completed more than seventy years after work started on it, during the Civil War and the construction of several official buildings and ministries broke up the axial layouts designed to give permanent views of the two main seats of government.

In the early years of the 19th century the Mall was more or less empty too, to the extent that nothing and no-one prevented the construction in 1847 of the Smithsonian Institution, a romantic red-brick castle.

Furthermore, in 1872 permission was granted to the Baltimore and Potomac Railroad to place the railway station almost next door to the Capitol, where in 1906 Daniel H. Burnham's monumental Union Station was to rise.
Burnham was actually the author, in 1901, of the second plan (officially named after Senator James McMillan, president of the commission for the District of Columbia)

28 top Washington Cathedral, built in Gothic style, was begun in 1907 and only finished in 1990.

28-29 The white outline of the Capitol and its cupola stand out on the long avenue of the Mall. The cupola is covered in steel sheets which are periodically repainted white. It takes about three tons of white paint each time.

29 top The Islamic Center, built in 1995 to plans designed by the architect Mario Rossi, is one of the most important Islamic buildings in the United States.

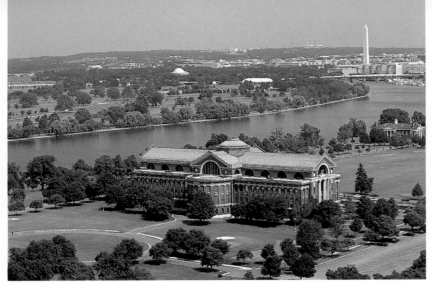

which attempted to define the urban image of Washington by completing L'Enfant's plan. Burnham used to say that small plans would not excite the minds of men, and for Washington he did indeed design something on a grand scale: the Mall's L-shape design was enhanced, extending the two arms and thereby creating a crossroads.

The Capitol and the White House stood at the existing western and southern extremities while the monument to Lincoln was placed on the new eastern arm (extended further with the bridge over the Potomac towards Arlington) and to the north with a memorial chapel to the Heroes of the Revolution (later reduced to the Jefferson Memorial). It was intended to evict the Smithsonian and the railway from the Mall and move the obelisk in memory of Washington (which subsidence problems had made impossible to align perfectly) and create big avenues and parks to emphasise the capital's monumental appearance. Although this plan met with great success, it too was only partly followed as healthy American pragmatism saved the turreted Smithsonian and prevented the spending of a fortune to realign the monument to the first president.

The attention and importance given right from the very beginning to the capital's parks and gardens by the town's planners — Thomas Jefferson, who in addition to being a politician and architect was also a landscape gardener and L'Enfant himself, who took the gardens of Versailles as his inspiration — had luckier results. Washington is today the only city whose maps include rows of trees marked by name; it boasts huge areas covered with gardens, fountains and flowerbeds as well as immense parks like Rock Creek (a park and nature reserve with more than twenty kilometres of footpaths in an almost uncontaminated environment, in which the city's zoo is housed), the East Potomac Park, Constitution Gardens, with their lake covering almost seven acres and the amazing Dumbarton Oaks Park, designed by Beatrix Farrand, the first woman garden architect.

The capital's gardens, such as those around the White House — Lafayette Square and the wooded Ellipse in front of the

30 top left Potomac Park is one of Washington's main green areas.

30 top right Mount Vernon, near the capital, is the estate where George Washington lived and died.

30-31 Seen from above, the Thomas Jefferson Memorial clearly reveals its debt to the third president's architectonic taste. Its circular plan is directly derived from Pantheon in Rome.

31 top The Robert F. Kennedy Memorial Stadium boasts seating for 55,000 and is the home ground of one of the capital's sporting glories, the Washington Redskins football team. The stadium also periodically hosts wrestling and boxing contests, concerts, circuses, rodeos and Disney on Ice.

presidential residence — as well as the Botanic Gardens, whose 19th-century glasshouse stands in front of the Capitol, fill well-defined roles and have definite identities, constituting something more that the natural complement to a building or a monument. They have an identity and a "scenic presence", plenty of which is also to be found in the city's official buildings. The foremost of these is the Capitol, the seat of Congress, the St.Peter's (and the dome harks back to Rome's basilica) of any pilgrimage to Washington. Designed by a doctor, William Thornton, built on a hill at the end of the Mall, its foundation stone laid by the father of the country, George Washington, on 18th September 1793, like others of the capital's buildings, it was ravaged by fire set by the British troops in 1814 and was only completed in 1863. If the Capitol constitutes the city's focal point, with the Rotunda, its cupola frescoed by Costantino Brumidi with the Apotheosis of Washington, Statuary Hall crowded with the effigies of the most illustrious citizens of the United States of America and the chambers of the Senate and of the House of Representatives, the White House is the catalyst of the hopes and fears of the nation and of the entire world. A somewhat modest seat of power, this pure white Georgian-style house was designed as the President's official residence in 1790 (and completed in 1829) by James Hoban, an Irish architect, to be comfortable but not opulent and to invoke admiration but not fear in the citizenry, who still visit some of the 132 rooms with religious composure today. Its main office measures 57 metres by 27, nothing compared to similar examples, such as Buckingham Palace. The Treasury Building, situated on the right of the White House and erected like most of the big federal administrative buildings during the 19th century, is an opulent Grecian temple, all columns, marbles and capitals, dedicated to the dollar god. The austere, classical, lines of the temple which houses the seat of judicial power, the Supreme Court, preceded by a magnificent setting of sweeping steps, dates from 1935. The same year, John Russell Pope designed the Corinthian columns which surround the National Archives

32 top The celebrated Oval Office, the President's private office, is where decisions affecting the destinies not just of the nation, but of the entire world are made.

32-33 The official residence of the President of the United States since 1st November 1800, when John and Abigail Adams moved in, the White House — seen here from the western side — was built as the result of a public competition, which offered prize money of $500. Thomas Jefferson entered using a pseudonym.

33 top Lafayette Square is the name given to the formal gardens on the north side of the White House. It was George Washington's idea in 1785 to buy the then orchard belonging to Mr. Pierce's farm, in order to turn it into a public park with exotic and indigenous plants. The National Park Service organises open-air concerts here in the summer.

34-35 The White House, oldest of the capital's government buildings, has been the residence of every American president with the exception of George Washington. Designed by James Hoban, it was initially called President House and then the Executive Mansion, only taking on its current name in 1902.

36-37 The Supreme Court, the highest court in the United States, was housed from 1810-1860 in the cellars of the Capitol building. Its powers include that of legislative veto, ruling on unconstitutionality and the interpretation of the constitution. Its decisions can only be altered by the Court itself.

The building, which is located to the east of the Capitol, also houses a statue of John Marshall and a small museum dedicated entirely to the history of this fundamental institution. Around 150 people can sit in on the Court's sessions at a time and its calendar is published in the Washington Post.

building. The Baths of Diocletian and Constantine's Arch in Rome are the model for the Union Station, the 1908 railway station which now houses shops and restaurants, while the Masonic Temple of the Scottish Rite, also designed by Pope in 1910, was inspired by the Tomb of Halicarnassus.

The area known as the Federal Triangle dates from the 1930s. This is a kilometre of federal offices with prevalently classical facades, which include amongst others the neo-Romantic Pavilion at the Old Post Office (now a mall) and the modern FBI headquarters. The use of classical forms for the buildings which made up monumental Washington continued for over one and a half centuries right up to the west wing of the National Gallery, designed by Pope in 1941.

It was only with Dulles Airport, designed in 1962 by E. Saarinen and the triangular module of the National Gallery's east wing, designed in 1978 by I.M.Pei, that the capital was able to boast examples of the best in contemporary architecture.

If Washington is the politicians' capital, Arlington is the fief of the military. Suburban Arlington, connected to the Lincoln Memorial by the Arlington Memorial Bridge over the Potomac, is in fact the home of the National Cemetery, reserved for the military, both officers and other ranks. This is where the Gracchi of the United States are laid to rest, President John F. Kennedy and Senator Robert Kennedy; here is the Doric colonnade of Arlington House, the residence of the Confederate general, Robert E. Lee, preceded by the simple tomb of Major Pierre L'Enfant.

A simple white sarcophagus, containing the remains of four unknown servicemen, marks the Tomb of Unknowns, where a moving Changing of the Guard ceremony is performed. Official commemorative ceremonies take place in the Memorial Amphitheatre. But Arlington, site now of Washington National Airport too, is not just an immense monument to the past. It is also home to the emblem of the United States ' power today, the massive Pentagon, which houses the Department of Defense: 23,000 military and civilian employees, 17 and a half miles of corridors, 7,754

38 top The Corcoran Gallery of Art, set up in 1869, has been housed since 1897 in the building designed by Ernest Flagg. The collection exhibits the personal collection of the banker and philanthropist William Wilson Corcoran.

38-39 The sober headquarters of the American Red Cross are housed in a building in classical architectural style dating from 1917 and situated to the south of the Corcoran Gallery.

windows and 691 drinking fountains to quench their thirst. The life which was frozen and imprisoned by the Mall's monumentality seems to have withdrawn to the suburbs and to the fashionable districts. From Foggy Bottom, down by the river, with the State Department, George Washington University and the Kennedy Center, to the Bohemian residential district of Dupont Circle, home of artists, elegant Victorian houses and one of the country's most influential gay communities; from Adams-Morgan with its wealth of ethnic influences, to the multiform Downtown, with the buildings of the Federal Triangle and the lawyers' offices on K Street, right along to the exclusive Georgetown, home of journalists, civil servants and professionals and to Embassy Row where, as it names suggests, all the embassies are located, Washington today has plenty to offer, especially to its residents.

Even if the city is divided between Democrats and Republicans and, with the exception of the Capitol Hill district, blacks live to the east of 16th Street and whites to the west, support for the local football team, the Redskins, the spectacular Japanese Cherry Blossom Festival at the Tidal Basin lake and the grandiose national parades held on majestic Pennsylvania Avenue arouse the enthusiasm of all Washingtonians. Georgetown is particularly loved by its inhabitants as the place where Washington plays at being a town, before a capital city. Terminus of the C&O Canal, with the old port for the tobacco and cereal trades, cobbled streets, the old university, brick sidewalks and the small Georgian-style houses, this oldest of the city's residential sites is also the youngest and liveliest and has earned itself the name of the St. Germain-des-Prés of the United States. The C&O Canal itself is immensely popular.

Its 295 kilometres were dug out between 1828-1850 to connect Georgetown to Cumberland and its historical national park attracts more than 6,000,000 visitors every year — joggers, canoeists and cyclists alike.

There are historical sites all along the canal route: Antietam, the site of an important Civil War battle, the 18th-century

39 top The Old Post Office, the oldest federal building in the city, has been converted into one of the most popular of Washington's shopping malls. Thanks to strong public protest in the 1930s, the building escaped its planned demolition and has been returned, albeit with a new function, to its former splendour.

40 The headquarters of the OAS, the Organization of American States, is considered one of the capital's most handsome buildings. The building, which is also known as the House of the Americas, includes the Aztec Garden, with its wealth of fountains and exotic plants like coffee, cocoa, date palms and the so-called bread tree. It also houses the Tree of Peace, a ficus planted in 1910 by President Taft and the statue of the Aztec god of flowers, Xochipilli.

40-41 Constitution Hall is one of the best-known historical buildings in Washington; it houses the venerable association of the Daughters of the American Revolution, with a membership of still 200,000.

Fort Frederick and Harper's Ferry, scene of John Brown's anti-slavery revolt in 1859 and the panorama of Great Falls. Another traditional destination for Washington visitors is the town of Alexandria, which conservation projects carried out over the period from 1961 to 1981 have restored to its original 18th-century appearance. Founded on the right bank of the Potomac by Scottish colonists around the middle of the 18th century, its importance was founded on the tobacco trade. As a result of its closeness to the capital (only 14 kilometres) it rivals Georgetown as a residential district and a shopping centre and for its historic buildings and small eighteenth-century houses.

The last compulsory stop, in order to grasp the historical atmosphere which surrounds the capital fully, is Mount Vernon, around 25 kilometres south of the capital, the estate where George Washington lived and died. In addition to the main building which houses memorabilia and furniture, the tombs of the president and his wife are on the banks of the Potomac, the river which laps many of the most important monuments in Washington — a watery umbilical cord linking the father of the nation to his capital, which even death has not been able to cut.

41 top The neo-classical Treasury Building, built in 1842-69, is currently the headquarters of the Treasury Department.

42-43 The photograph shows the National Archives and the Exhibition Hall's central rotunda with cupola, where some of the most significant original documents in American history are on permanent show: the Declaration of Independence (4th July 1776), the Constitution of the United States (17th September 1787) and the Bill of Rights (1789, partially ratified two years later). Since 1984 visitors have also been able to admire an authentic copy of the English Magna Charta, dating from 1297, found in 1974.

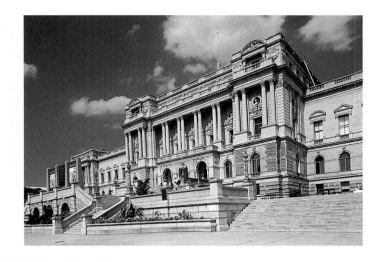

44 top The fountain of Neptune decorates the Thomas Jefferson Building, the oldest and most important of the buildings which comprise the library. Behind this is the John Adams Building, built in 1939, and the modern white marble James Madison Memorial Building, added on to the southern side of the main building in 1980. The rare exhibits on show at the Library of Congress include one of the three extant copies of Gutenberg's Bible, printed in 1455 and the Mainz Bible, an illuminated manuscript dating from 1452-53. The library owns, amongst others, documents which belonged to Freud as well as Houdini's magic books, and ten new books are added every minute.

45 top left The facade of the Thomas Jefferson Building was built in 1886-97 in Italian Renaissance style and was intended to hold the Congress library which had been instituted in 1800 with an allocation of $5000 and then destroyed in 1814 by the British.

45 top right The spectacular Main Reading Room, a huge circular room topped by a cupola, houses the catalogues and reading places.

44-45 and 45 bottom The ceiling of the Great Hall is richly decorated and echoes the neo-classical themes which characterise the building.

46-47 Academic classicism, the most characteristic style of federal architecture in Washington, reaches one of its highest forms of expression in the Supreme Court building. The massive staircase, the three-floor-high portico formed from a double row of eight Corinthian columns, the bronze doors with sculpted bas-reliefs and the four internal courtyards dressed in white Georgian marble, are all inspired by the solemnity of the basilicas of Ancient Rome.

48 The J.F. Kennedy Center for the Performing Arts is the work of architect E.D. Stone and was inaugurated in 1971. It was extended in 1978 by Philip Johnson and John Burgee. The modern building, which is reflected in the waters of the Potomac, has halls for concerts, ballets and areas for theatre. It is also home to the National Symphony Orchestra and the American Film Institute.

49 A shot of the Grand Foyer on the ground floor. The size of two football pitches, it has picture windows looking out over the river and unique crystal chandeliers. In the middle of the room is the much-admired bronze bust of John F. Kennedy, the work of Robert Berks.

50-51 The Pentagon, with its unmistakable five-sided shape, is the emblem of American military power. Headquarters of the Defense Department, it lies outside the District of Columbia city limits, at Arlington. Built between the years 1941 and 1943 to plans by the architect George E. Bergstrom (working together with the U.S. Army Corps of Engineers), it is five storeys high, has 7,754 windows and 23,000 people, civilians and military, are employed there.

52-53 The Columbus Memorial Fountain is located in the square next to Union Station, the main Washington railway station. Built in 1908, it was an example of the optimism which characterised the Roosevelt era. In 1988 it was restructured and transformed in part into a shopping mall, with restaurants, cafés, shops and nine movie and stage theatres.

52 top The colourful Friendship Arch in Chinatown is situated north of the Old Patent Office Building. The unique construction was put up in 1986 thanks to funds supplied by the federal government and the capital city of the People's Republic of China, Beijing.

52 bottom The Old Post Office was the first of the town's government buildings to have a clock tower. Designed by the architect Willoghby Edbrook in Victorian style, it was restructured by Arthur Cotton Moore Associates with light-supplying windows replacing the aluminium covering of the central courtyard and since 1984 has been a meeting-point for tourists on the Mall.

53 top The Capitol South station on the subway has a continuous coffered roof in cement which is quite unmistakable, giving an idea of solidity and of opulence at the same time. Defined in "Fortune" magazine as a solid-gold Cadillac for mass-transportation, it has been open since 1976. It was designed by the architect Harry Weese and has four lines.

54-55 View of the Old Executive Office Building, situated close to the White House. Built in granite between 1871 and 1888, by the architect Alfred B. Mullett, to house the State, War and Navy Departments, its main theme is that of an imaginative reworking of the Beaux Arts style. It was here after the attack on Pearl Harbour that the Secretary of State, Cordell Hull, met the representatives of the Japanese government.

54 top and 55 Columbia Road is one of the busiest roads in the Bohemian, trendy part of town known as Adams Morgan, north of Dupont Circle. Full of night clubs, bars and restaurants which offer cuisine from all parts of the world, it is considered, along with Georgetown, to be the heart of the capital's night-life. Its multi-ethnic population is composed of Hispanic, Central American, African and Asian immigrants.

56-57 The Botanic Gardens, with their huge greenhouse designed in the 19th-century style of Kew Gardens and Syon Park in England, by Bennett, Parsons and Frost, are situated close to the Capitol.

56 top and 57 top The Bishop's Garden is one of the capital's most attractive corners. From the door of the southern transept of Washington Cathedral at the bottom of Wisconsin Avenue, to the intersection with Massachusetts Avenue, visitors have access to a series of rose gardens and smaller gardens rich in magnolias and herbs. There are also glasshouses for growing rare species. Thomas Jefferson, a passionate landscaper and gardener, as well as a politician, was the inspiration for the many parks and gardens which constitute one of the American capital's greatest sources of pride.

57 bottom Created in 1882 to provide housing for a large collection of plants from the Southern Seas, the Botanic Gardens hold more than 8,000 species and varieties. The amazing spring flowering of tulips is a must and particularly popular in the capital, so are the azaleas. The tropical sectors, the succulents and the cacti are particular interesting and the orchid house has varieties in flower practically all the year round.

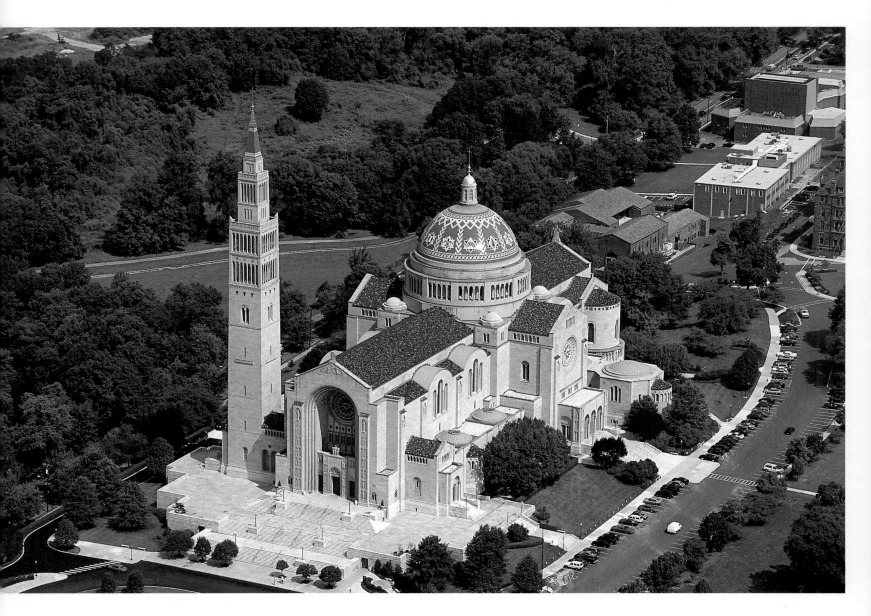

58. The imposing National Shrine of the Immaculate Conception, the sanctuary situated in the north-eastern part of Washington, is considered the largest Roman Catholic church in the Unite States. It has 57 chapels, can hold over 6,000 worshippers and was built in Romanesque-Byzantine style between 1920 and 1959. It is 139 metres long by 100 metres high, with a mighty bell-tower inspired by the one in St. Mark's Square in Venice, and a blue and gold cupola.

59 St. Peter's Roman Catholic church, one of the capital's many places of worship, shows that Washington is a multi-ethnic and cosmopolitan city in religious matters too. There are 830 churches in the city at the moment, many of which are situated on 16th Street, as well as convents, seminaries and other religious foundations.

60-61 Views from inside the Washington National Cathedral of St. Peter and St. Paul, the sixth largest in the world, on Mount St. Alban in the District of Columbia: the buildings, which has more than 320 stone angels and 200 stained-glass windows, was built to a design by George F. Bodley and Henry Vaughan and was later enlarged by Philip Hubert Frohman.
It has three naves with side chapels, a large transept, choir and ambulatory.
In the right-hand nave there is the Space Window, into which a piece of moon rock brought back to earth in 1969 by the crew of Apollo 11 has been inserted. The foundation stone came from Bethlehem and the stones used for the pulpit from Canterbury Cathedral. President Woodrow Wilson is buried here.

62-63 The grandiose Union Station, created by the architect Daniel H. Burnham, a leading exponent of the Beaux Arts style. He drew his inspiration from the Constantine's Arch for the portico and the Baths of Diocletian for the interior. Presidents Taft, Wilson and Roosevelt used to receive foreign diplomats in the Presidential Suite here; this is where Rear-Admiral Byrd arrived, after his expedition to the South Pole and where the body of Franklin Delano Roosevelt arrived in 1945. In 1907 it cost the then astronomical figure of $30 million; in the 1950s the station fell into disuse as a result of the decline in rail traffic and was saved from inevitable destruction by an act of Congress in 1981. It was restructured at a cost of $160 million and although it maintained its original function, it was transformed into one of the capital's most popular meeting places.

64-65 Pictures of the huge parade which takes place through the heart of the capital to celebrate Independence Day on 4th July. This is one of the best-loved of American holidays and Washington residents organise picnics along the banks of the Potomac. The day ends with a fantastic firework show. The Independence Day parades' route includes Pennsylvania Avenue, the long diagonal artery which links the Capitol to the White House. The main axis of the grandiose plan devised for the new capital in 1791 by the French architect Pierre-Charles L'Enfant and never fully completed, this avenue is also known as the Main Street of the U.S. With its torrid summer climate and extremely cold winters, Washington was not very popular and had a small population, in fact at the beginning of the 20th century its inhabitants numbered only 300,000. It was the increase in the clerical classes and the creation of the military bureaucracy in the 1930s which gave it its international character, so that around the middle of the century it reached its historic peak: 800,000 residents.

66-67 During the year Washington is a stage for several important events, like the Festival of American Folklife, dedicated to craft, music and good. The festival, which is promoted by the Smithsonian Institution, takes place on the Mall every year, during the last days of June and the beginning of July. Another regular event is the Hispanic-American Cultural Festival, which is held in summer in the multi-ethnic district of Adams Morgan and where music, dance and art are all on display. The same district also has its own folk festival on Adams-Morgan Day in September.

68 Freedom Plaza with is fountain, is dominated on its eastern side by the statue of the Polish general Kazimierz Pulaski who took part in the War of Independence and was fatally wounded in 1779 at the siege of Savannah. The paving in the square, also known as Western Plaza, have the town plan drawn up in 1791 by Pierre L'Enfant.

69 The proposal to erect a monument to the memory of Abraham Lincoln gave rise to a long debate. Some wanted to raise a second obelisk alongside Washington's, others wanted a pyramid and some simply wanted a public park. Some also supported the idea of building a huge commemorative road linking Washington to Gettysburg, where Lincoln pronounced the celebrated Gettysburg Address.

70-71 and 71 top Wisconsin Avenue is one of the main shopping roads in Georgetown. Today this residential district of Washington, which grew out of an old town pre-dating the foundation of the capital city, has elegant restaurants, shops, historic houses and boutiques. Having originally grown up in the 18th century around a flourishing tobacco port, it declined at the end of the last century, but expanded again in the 1930s, becoming on of the capital's favourite shopping districts.

71 bottom M Street in Georgetown runs parallel to the Chesapeake and Ohio Canal, which was excavated between 1828 and 1850, to link the city with Pittsburgh. However, it was never completed and stopped at Cumberland, 184 miles north-west. The road has some of the finest examples of early 19th-century buildings and also boasts the district's oldest building, the Old Stone House. Erected in 1765 by the cabinet-maker Christopher Layman, it was bought by Cassandra Chew and turned into an ale-house and then, in the 1940s, into a garage. It was acquired by the National Park Service in 1950, restored and opened to the public.

72 top and 72-73 Wisconsin Avenue and M Street are the most interesting roads in Georgetown, with plenty of Victorian buildings, fashionable shops, night clubs and restaurants. The inhabitants of this old district prefer to maintain their tranquillity and a few years ago voted against the arrival of the subway. It is the preferred district of, journalists and diplomats who live in Washington. It is also the home of the oldest Roman Catholic University in the country, Georgetown University, founded in 1789.

73 Georgetown, to the west of the District of Columbia and officially known as West Washington, is characterised by the presence of small houses built in the last century, often brightly coloured, brick pavements and tiny yards. Many streets are still cobbled, some have gas lamps and many houses bear black plaques indicating that they are places of historic interest. The price of houses in Georgetown rises with the arrival of a Democrat in the White House and fall when the Republicans get in, as the latter tend to look down on this rather Bohemian area and prefer the suburbs.

74-75 Washington speaks two different architectural languages. In the Mall, which is the centre of government, a classical style prevails, with majestic buildings nonchalantly copied from Greek and Roman models, while eclecticism holds sway in the rest of the city. However, the relative value of the buildings is amply compensated by the huge parks, the sheer size of the open spaces and the fine road layout, based on the two right-angled axes of the Mall which hinge on the most significant monuments and a rational road system. The system is made less linear by the radial avenues designed by l'Enfant. At the beginning of this century, the McMillan plan was developed and the Mall's two arms were extended, producing a cross-shaped layout.

76 top Il C&O Canal
(Chesapeake and Ohio Canal)
was dug between 1828 and
1850 to connect the city to
Pittsburg; its design was not
fully achieved since the
excavation works stopped at
Cumberland, 184 miles
north-west.

76-77 Washington Harbour at Georgetown is built in post-modern style and has restaurants, offices and apartments. Downriver from here the Watergate building, the setting for the scandal which took its name, and the Kennedy Center are both visible. Founded by Scottish immigrants along the banks of the rive Potomac (from the native American word Powtowmac, which means teeming with fish), Georgetown received its town charter in 1749. It took its current name in 1789. It had previously, from 1751, been called simply George, in honour of George II of England. From the end of the 18th century onwards, numerous bridges were built to link the town to the southern bank of the river and therefore to Virginia.

78-79 A lift takes visitors up to the observatory on the Washington Monument, 152 metres up, to look out on one of the finest views of the District of Columbia and a piece of Maryland and Virginia.
The US capital, officially inaugurated in 1800, immediately had the opportunity to ennoble itself by linking its name to the father of the Republic and first President of the United States, George Washington, who died in December 1799. However, this did not prevent the monument dedicated to him remaining incomplete for many years through lack of funds, until in 1876 Congress allocated $200,000 for its completion, carried out by the Army Corps of Engineers. Four years after the work was finished, in 1884, the monument was opened to the public.

80 top The ceremony of the changing of the guard in front of the Tomb of the Unknowns in Arlington National Cemetery, the white sarcophagus is the work of the sculptor Thomas Hudson Jones, takes place every half an hour from April to September, every hour the rest of the year and every hour during the night. The tomb contains the remains of four unknown servicemen who fell during the Ist World War, the 2nd World War, the Korean War and the Vietnam War respectively.

80-81 and 81 top and bottom The Memorial Amphitheater at Arlington National Cemetery, built by the architects Carrere and Hastings, is the setting for the official commemorative ceremonies for the fallen held on special days like Memorial Day or Veterans Day. The neo-classical building, which dates from 1920, recalls the form of the amphitheatres of the ancient world. Close by to it are the monument to the astronauts who died in the explosion of the space Shuttle Challenger in 1986 and those who died in Iran in 1980, during the attempt to free the American Embassy hostages.

82-83 An eternal flame burns in the cemetery at Arlington on the tomb of John F. Kennedy, killed in Dallas in 1963. His tomb is one of the unrelinquishable sites for visitors to the capital.

82 bottom. Close to the tomb of J.F.K. is a plaque and a simple white cross marking the burial place of Robert F. Kennedy, who was assassinated in 1968.

82 top and 83 top The tomb of the elder of the Kennedy brothers is at the feet of the hill where Arlington House, also known as Custis-Lee Mansion, stands, with its majestic Doric portico. The 19th-century building originally belonged to G.W.P. Custis, nephew of Washington's second wife Mary Ann, whose daughter married General Robert E. Lee.

84-85 There are almost 200,000 graves in the cemetery at Arlington, a suburb of Washington, which holds the remains of military and civilian government personnel as well as those of the boxer Joe Louis and the actor Lee Marvin. The first soldier to be buried there was William Christman, who died of peritonitis during the Civil War, in 1864.

The town is part of Arlington County and once belonged to the District of Columbia, but was rejoined to Virginia in 1864. Arlington is also home to the Pentagon, the Defense Department and Washington National Airport. The capital has another airport, Dulles International Airport, designed by Eero Saarinen.

THE MONUMENTS

Washington is not only accepted to be the richest of all American cities in terms of museums, art galleries, cultural and scientific attractions, it also has the most monuments. Generals, politicians, orators, men of culture: they all are here, behind this solemn and composed front, ready to fight it out with marble, staircases, fountains and scenic vistas, vying for the visitors' admiration. Ready to mortgage the future, each defending not just their memory, but their fame and their place in the history books. In the parks and the rotundas, between lakes or in official buildings, statues, cenotaphs and plaques celebrate the fathers of the nation and their virtues. From the Peace Monument to the Freedmen's Memorial (dedicated in 1876 to Abraham

Lincoln and erected with donations from ex-slaves), from the statue of the Marquis de Lafayette to that of the Count de Rochambeau or General Sheridan, a tour of the capital's monuments is a rapid revision course of the epic deeds of the United States of America. The place chosen for this ideal pantheon is, of course, the imposing Mall, dominated by the beacon of American civilisation, the Washington Monument — a homage to the man but, above all, to the nation which generated him.

Surely, no-one else has been so absolutely venerated, so completely frozen, in legend, according to Marcus Cunliffe in his 1958 publication "George Washington, Man and Monument". In fact, when it came to this man, leader in battle and first president, the man who, in the oft-cited words of Henry Lee was the first in war, the first in peace and the first in the hearts of his countrymen, the United States could not resist the opportunity to give rein to greatness and rhetoric and dedicated this huge white obelisk, 169 metres of Maryland marble, to him. Erected in December 1884 to a design by Robert Mills, the monument was supposed to be sited on the axis of the Capitol, but subsidence in the area allocated for the construction meant it had to be moved about a hundred metres out of the Mall's line of perspective.

86 $500 was the prize fixed in 1792 by the Commission for the competition for the Capitol. Due to the winner's (Dr. William Thornton) obvious lack of expertise, first the French architect Stephen Hallett and then Benjamin A. Latrobe were appointed to oversee the construction work. In 1818 the American Charles Bullfinch took over, followed by Robert Mills and Thomas U. Walter, who was responsible for the building we see today.
More than seventy years were to pass between the laying of the foundation stone in a Masonic ritual by George Washington and the conclusion of the works.

87 The architect Pierre-Charles L'Enfant had arrived as a volunteer in the United States from France to fight in the War of Independence. He intended the monument to George Washington to be placed at the intersection of the two large axes comprising gardens in front of the White House and the Capitol, which are marked on his original plan with the names President Palace and Congress House, and it should have been an equestrian statue.

88-89 Thomas Jefferson was an extremely cultured man. He had been a lawyer, knew Latin and Greek, read Homer, Tacitus, Cicero and Horace. He played the violin and loved mathematics, natural sciences and botany and possessed the most important architectural library in the country. As Governor of Virginia, then Secretary of State and then President of the United States, he took steps to push the nation's ideas on architecture towards the models of the classical ages, especially Ancient Rome. During the eight years of his presidency, from 1800 to 1808, art and culture thrived amazingly. Few presidents did so much to give the newborn capital an identity and he not only defined the classical style of the government buildings, but tried to preserve the natural heritage of old woods too.

It does however still provide a splendid view of the latter from the top of its observatory. Just as with the Ancient Egyptians, the obelisk pays homage to a man who during his lifetime was the object of a cult almost equalling that of a god (as early as 1775, many children were being named after him). A man who after his death seemed to encompass all the American virtues, so much so, that one state, seven mountains, eight rivers, ten lakes, 33 provinces and 121 towns and cities, first and foremost Federal City itself, are named after him. Thomas Jefferson, author of the American Declaration of Independence, Secretary of State and twice President, wrote at the beginning of the nineteenth century that architecture was his passion, building walls and knocking down walls were his favourite pastimes. To this lover of Palladio and of classicity, to "the first American who turned to Fine Art in order to build a shelter from inclement weather" (Chastellux), to the owner of the largest collection of books on architecture in the country, to the man who influenced the architectonic conception of the capital, urging it towards the forms of Republican Rome, Washington pays homage with the last strictly neo-classical monument in the city: the Jefferson Memorial. The Memorial, erected in 1943 by John Russell Pope, reflects Jefferson's preference for classical shapes and harks back to the Palladian forms of Monticello, his private residence and the Rotunda of the University of Virginia, Charlottesville, which he designed. The waters of the Tidal Basin, the artificial lake connected to the Potomac, which in April is decked out with the magnificent flowering of hundreds of Japanese cherry trees, create an imposing mirror image of the pantheon's Ionic colonnade in white Georgian marble, under which Rudolph Evans's bronze statue (5.8 metres high) of the illustrious Virginian is sited.

The Greek temple of the Lincoln Memorial, sited in West Potomak Park on the same axis as the Capitol, is characterised by severe Doric columns. Surely one of the best-known American monuments, it was designed in 1922 by Henry Bacon and is mirrored in the Reflecting Pool, the

90-91 Author of the Declaration of Independence of the United States, founder of the University of Virginia, in 1786 Thomas Jefferson, inspired by the Roman temple at Nimes (also known as the Maison Carrée) which he had admired during a journey to the South of France in 1787, designed the Capitol building at Richmond. During that tour he also spent a short time in northern Italy, and wrote to the Countess of Tessé that from Lyons to Nimes he fed upon the remains of the greatness of Rome. He was immersed in antiquity from morning to evening. For him Rome really existed in all the splendour of its empire. He was alarmed by the attacks of the Goths, the Visigoths, the Ostrogoths and the Vandals, fearing that they would lead back to the original barbarity.

92 The Reflecting Pool, the scenic corridor of water 600 metres long, which mirrors the Washington Monument to the east and the Lincoln Memorial to the west, was designed by Henry Bacon and Charles McKim in 1920, to lighten the long empty space of the Mall. It is now one of the capital's most popular meeting places, used for model boat races in the summer and ice-skating in the winter.

93 The Lincoln Memorial, situated in the West Potomac Park, is one of the many monuments dedicated by the American capital city to his presidents and heroes. The Theodore Roosevelt Memorial, built on the island of the same name and the General Grant Memorial, on the Capitol hill are an example. The last is a sculptural group with the equestrian statue of the General at its center, realized by Henry Schrady in 1922.

impressive 600-metre long tract of water (designed in 1920 by Bacon and Charles McKim), at whose other end the Washington Monument rises. In the atrium of the Memorial opening on to the Mall, is the giant, white marble, statue of the seated president, thoughtful but resolute, paternal but not severe.

Open to visitors all year round, day and night, the Lincoln Memorial is the site of an unceasing flow of "pilgrims" come to pay homage to the man who in 1865 paid with his life for incarnating a nation's ideals of equality and liberty.

It is by no means coincidental that it was on these steps, from which on a clear night you can see the flame burning on the tomb at Arlington of another assassinated president, John F. Kennedy, that in 1969 Martin Luther King pronounced his famous speech "I have a dream", with which he shouted to the world his dream of a nation of free and equal men. Washington does not forget.

94-95 The four equestrian statues which decorate Arlington Memorial Bridge, which was built to span the river Potomac in 1926-32 to link the Lincoln Memorial to the town of Arlington, were donated to the city of Washington by Italy in 1951. Of the city's many bridges, Buffalo Bridge (1914) in Rock Creek Park – which looks like a Roman viaduct and is decorated with a series of sculptures of Indian heads and four massive buffalo sculpted by A. Phimister Proctor – and Connecticut Avenue Bridge, decorated with eight monumental urns and also in Creek Park, are worthy of note.

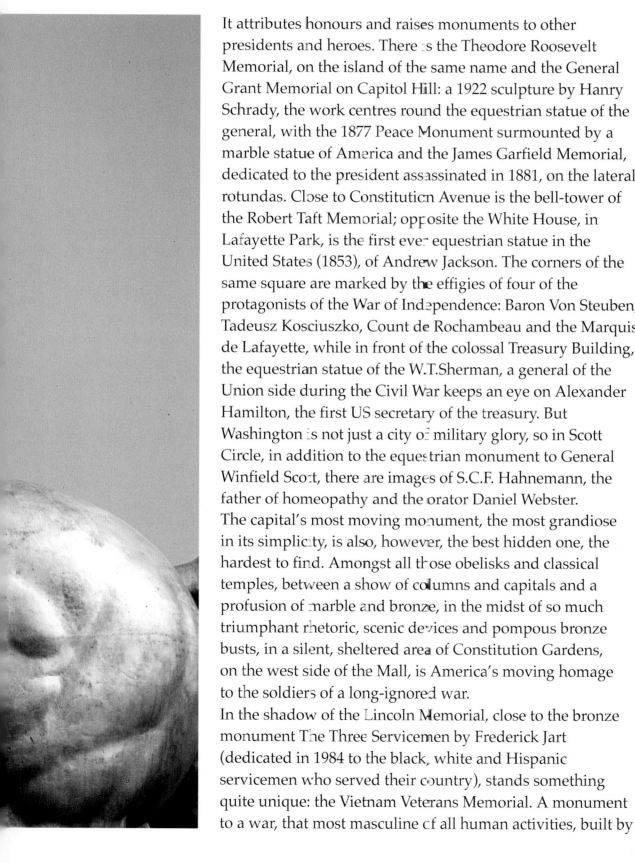

It attributes honours and raises monuments to other presidents and heroes. There is the Theodore Roosevelt Memorial, on the island of the same name and the General Grant Memorial on Capitol Hill: a 1922 sculpture by Hanry Schrady, the work centres round the equestrian statue of the general, with the 1877 Peace Monument surmounted by a marble statue of America and the James Garfield Memorial, dedicated to the president assassinated in 1881, on the lateral rotundas. Close to Constitution Avenue is the bell-tower of the Robert Taft Memorial; opposite the White House, in Lafayette Park, is the first ever equestrian statue in the United States (1853), of Andrew Jackson. The corners of the same square are marked by the effigies of four of the protagonists of the War of Independence: Baron Von Steuben, Tadeusz Kosciuszko, Count de Rochambeau and the Marquis de Lafayette, while in front of the colossal Treasury Building, the equestrian statue of the W.T.Sherman, a general of the Union side during the Civil War keeps an eye on Alexander Hamilton, the first US secretary of the treasury. But Washington is not just a city of military glory, so in Scott Circle, in addition to the equestrian monument to General Winfield Scott, there are images of S.C.F. Hahnemann, the father of homeopathy and the orator Daniel Webster. The capital's most moving monument, the most grandiose in its simplicity, is also, however, the best hidden one, the hardest to find. Amongst all those obelisks and classical temples, between a show of columns and capitals and a profusion of marble and bronze, in the midst of so much triumphant rhetoric, scenic devices and pompous bronze busts, in a silent, sheltered area of Constitution Gardens, on the west side of the Mall, is America's moving homage to the soldiers of a long-ignored war.
In the shadow of the Lincoln Memorial, close to the bronze monument The Three Servicemen by Frederick Jart (dedicated in 1984 to the black, white and Hispanic servicemen who served their country), stands something quite unique: the Vietnam Veterans Memorial. A monument to a war, that most masculine of all human activities, built by

95 The statues which adorn the Potomac Parkway, the long avenue along the river, maintain the same classical style as the ones on the Arlington Memorial Bridge.

96-97 Famous assemblies took place in the Lincoln Memorial. On its staircase, in 1969 Martin Luther King, the champion of the equality between black and white people, held his famous speech "I have dream".

98-99 The Marine Corps War Memorial, also known as the Iwo Jima Memorial, located close to Arlington National Cemetery, is dedicated to American Marines killed in war. The group of bronze figures, 23 metres high, upon design by Horace W. Peaslee and produced in 1954 by the sculptor Felix de Weldon, is taken from the famous photograph by the Pulitzer-prize winner, Joe Rosenthal: five sailors and marines raise the American flag on top of Mt. Suribachi in Japan, at the end of the battle fought in February 1945.

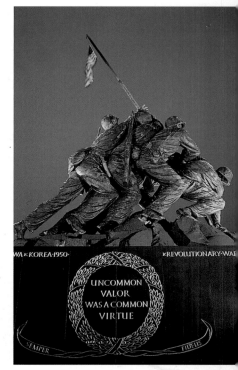

a woman; a monument to Vietnam created by a Chinese-American, Maya Ying Lin; a monument to the oldest of the world's pains designed by a Yale architecture student just 21 years old. A dark wound which rends the heart of the imperial capital of the New World Caesars, a monument free from rhetoric, driven with its pain like a wedge into the mother earth. So different from the proud reaching upwards which characterises the 23 metres of the Iwo Jima Memorial at Arlington, dedicated to the Marines who died in battle. The work of Felix W. De Weldon in 1954, based on Joe Rosenthal's famous photograph of the moment of victory: five soldiers raising the American flag on the top of Mount Suribachi in Japan, in February 1945.

From triumph to tragedy: the Vietnam Veterans Memorial, better known as the Wall, erected thanks to the pressure and private donations of Vietnam veterans, is a monument to the defeat, not just political, but social and cultural too, of an entire generation. Completed in 1982, it consists of a deep trench bordered by a long V-shaped wall of shiny black marble, its ends pointing to the Lincoln Memorial and the Washington Monument, on which the names of every person who fell or went missing in Vietnam from 1959 to 1975 are engraved in gold: 58,156 Americans. Fifty-eight thousand, one hundred and fifty six names which every year are stroked, bathed and touched by faces and hands which leave flowers and medals, press letters and little flags into the cracks; mirrored in the shiny, cold granite, they continue to feed this living monument and the dialogue which those no longer here. Despite everything, in Washington it is not the candid, icy monuments kissed by the sun or cradled by water which incarnate the soul, the heritage of ideals and civic virtues of this chamaeleon-like America — for that pure and adamantine soul shines here, in this black hole, smeared with earth, blood and pain. Here, where the shadow world mirrors and merges with the shadows of the living, by not denying this uncomfortable and lacerating past, this resounding defeat, the United States manages to find itself and the reasons for its greatness once again.

100 top The Korean War Veterans Memorial, erected to commemorate those who died in the bloody Korean War, was inaugurated in 1995. Situated in the little wood known as Ash Woods, it is between the Lincoln Memorial and Independence Avenue and is a line of soldiers marching towards an American flag.

100-101 Lafayette Square, in the centre of the park of the same name, is centred on the equestrian statue of Andrew Jackson which was made in 1853, the first to be cast in the United States. At the corners of the square are the images of four famous people who fought in the War of Independence: the Marquis Lafayette, the Count of Rochambeau, Tadeusz Kosciuszko and the Baron von Steuben.

101 top and bottom On 13th november 1984, a flagpole flying the American flag and a bronze sculpture by Frederick Hart, called The Three Servicemen, was erected next to the Vietnam Veterans Memorial. It is dedicated to the black, Caucasian and Hispanic soldiers who died serving their country.

102-103 One of the capital's most impressive monuments, the Vietnam Veterans Memorial is a long V-shaped wall of black marble. Thrust into the earth, it bears the names of almost sixty thousand American men and women, engraved in gold in chronological order, who died or went missing in the longest war ever fought by the United States and is situated between the Lincoln Memorial and the Washington Monument. Designed by the then 21-year architecture student, Maya Ying Lin, an Asian-American, it is better known simply as The Wall. It was inaugurated in 1982 and its cost, $7 million dollars, was paid for by private donations collected by the non-profit-making Vietnam Veteran's Memorial Fund, founded by Jan Scruggs.

104 -105 With the end of World War II and war-time restrictions on the use of metals, the large statue of Thomas Jefferson by Rudolph Evans was finally cast and the monument to the statesman thus completed. The completion of the final part of the construction, facing the Potomac, also marked the completion of the McMillan Plan, Daniel Burnham's great 19th-century project to reinforce the Mall's scenic setting with a cruciform layout. As had previously happened in the case of the Washington Memorial, the area chosen for this monument was unstable and a massive pile-sinking operation to a depth of 40 metres was necessary before the builders were sure that the land could support the weight of 54 Ionic columns and the building's marble walls.

BLACKMON Jr • CHARLES D StCLAIR REIN RODRIGUEZ • MARTIN JIM Jr • PA
JOHN H GEDDINGS • ALBERT L BROWN • WILLIAM H THIGPEN • JO
PERRY M SMITH • CECIL W SOUTHERLAND • MALCOLM J LYONS • DAVID W COON • JOHN L
JOSHUA M DANIELS • EUGENE T GILMORE • JOSEPH S TIDWELL • WILLIA
GLENN R ETHINGTON • JESUS A GONZALES • BILLY JOE PLASTER Jr
ARTHUR S NABBEN • JAMES F THAMES • HESSIE A BROOKS • JAMES R C ● RO
GREGORY S KARGER • RONALD D STEPHENSON • LOUIS W TRAVERS • R
• RONNIE G VAUGHAN • EUGENE J LEVICKIS • STEVEN W MOL
UGH D OPPERMAN • GREGORY L PEFFER • LARRY D BEAN • FRANK A CELA TO
• DONALD L SENTI • FREDERICK A VIGIL • MICHAEL H PETTY • DEN SO
• RONALD J REVIS • JAMES L COLWYE • ALFONSO A BRIT ER
RICHARD C PORTER • MERRELL E BRUMLEY Jr • WILLIAM O CREEC HUA
• JAMES P MARKEY Jr • WILLIAM D NICODEMUS • GEORGE L ROBE TS N
DEWIGHT E NORTON • STEVEN J OLCOTT • WILLIAM F REICHERT • JAMES V
• DEAN A HARRIS • RONALD M RIGDON • ARTHUR A SMITH • MI AE
DAVID I MIXTER • ROBERT L PULLIAM • JEFFREY L BAR
ALLEN C ELL • RAFAEL GARCIAPAGAN • RONALD W HA
HN R MILLER • ROBERT A SISK • JOHNNY C SPEARS • JOHNNY E TIVIS • PATRI
• JOSEPH W CASINO • CLYDE W COBLE • GORDON L CRAW E R
KEITH M JACKSON • WALTER X MENDEZ • THOMAS C MILLER STEPH
RICHARD D RANDOLPH • KEITH A STODDARD • MICHAEL P AUST N AR
FRANK S McCUTCHEON III • FLOYD RICHARDSON J
• LUTHER N BAGNAL III • MARTIN J BURNS • MILFRED R GREEN • LE AE
ROBERT L STANDERWICK Sr • JOSEPH L STONE • WALLIS W WEBB ERRE O
• JACKIE LEE DENNY • SAMUEL H EBERHART • GREGORY S SOMER
ANDRES LOPEZ RAMON • NELSON G RICHARDSON • DAYLE R HALL
CLIFTON E CALLAHAN • DAVID C JOHNSON • CLIFTON C NE
• RICHARD A WOODBURN • RICHARD A AARON • DAVI
CARL M WOOD • LARRY A WOODBURN • AMBERS A HAMILTON • ROBERT P
FRANK J GASPERICH Jr • AMBERS A HAMILTON • ROBERT P
• WILLIAM B RHODES • ROBERT J ROGERS • JOSEPH A TERESINSKI
BRIAN R FOLEY • THOMAS P B KING • RICHARD S KU
RUSSELL G BLOCHER • DONALD L MEEHAN Jr • CHARLES L PEACE • J SE
ROLAND D TROYANO • BRUCE A VAN DAM • CHAR ES E
LEWIS R YATES • ROLAND D TROYANO • CHARLES G BOB
THOMAS A SONY • RAFAEL RIVERA BENITEZ • MICHAE
LONALD R COLEMAN • THOMAS P DOODY • DALE
RANDALL L HARRIS • KEVIN P KNIGHT • CHARLES H SO
JOHN E ROBERTSON • BRUCE A CHRISTEN EVE
LENOX L RATCLIFF • GREG R CARTER • EDGAR McDANIEL STEPHE
GERAL J TWOREK • S BLACKBURN Jr • PHILLI SANDOVAL EPH
M N N PEARCE N NAL A MA EY
MELVIN J F ON RMAN J PE N ETH NY N
PAKELE JAMES F LLIN WHITE J SEPH R ANTH
CHARLES M CHARLES

STEPHEN R PHELPS · HARRY G PRINCE Jr
JUAN ESPINOSA · RAYMOND J GEORGE
JERRY W KIRKENDOLL · CHARLIE L LANIER
JAMES C MULLINAX Jr · STEVEN R PECK
CLYDE THOMAS · LLOYD W McCARTHY Jr
DUANE G HOWELL · CHARLES D ALLEN Jr
ENRIQUE ROSARIO SANTOS · RICHARD L BAUMAN
ROBERT C GREEN · STEPHEN R SCRIVENER
RONALD O SCHARNBERG · WILLIAM D SCHLUTTER
THOMAS E TESTORFF · RUSSELL G AHRENS
DAVID ELIZONDO · RICHARD W FORD · FREDERICK L CRISTMAN
THOMAS M KENNEDY · CAESAR MURRAY · GENE R KENNEDY
WILLIAM B BEARDSLEY · JOHN J CHUBB · DENNIS T DARLING
RONALD D KARAU · THOMAS E KINGSLEY · MICHAEL E KOSCHKE
VERNON G LOVE · RICK E McFARLAND · WILLIAM E ROYAL · JAMES D SCHOOLEY
MICHAEL D WOODARD · ALAN E DAVIS · DONALD J FRAZELLE · ERNEST L HIRTLER
JAMES W MANTHEI · BILLIE JAYE MARLING · LARRY M MASON · CLAUDIUS A SMALL
REGINALD J ABERNETHY · WILLIAM H FELLS · CHRISTOPHER Z CZARNOTA · TERRY W DOAN
BENJAMIN W DUNCAN · REGINALD D CLEVE · WILLIAM S GLENN · STEPHEN D GUCOFSKI
MICHAEL L HARRIS · DAVID R HAYWARD · DONALD P KNUTSEN · JEROME E LE ROY
ROBERT N LEBRUN · CHARLIE M LOGAN · PETER G MORIARTY · JOHN W McLEMORE Jr
CLARENCE M SUCHON · JOHN G TRAVER III · GARY S WHITE · THOMAS L ZEIGLER
MICHAEL J BOSILJEVAC · PAUL J FOTI · JESSIE J GARTH · JOHN D HEINZ · DENNIS M HOTALING
DONALD K OSBORN · JEFFERY I QUINTANILLA · LANCE A ROBINSON · WILLIAM L SCHELL
MANASSEH B WARREN · DOUGLAS E AYERS · CURTIS D BAUER · HARRY M BECKWITH III
JEROME D KLEIN · STEVEN M LARRABEE · JOHN C MERRITT · WILLIAM E NEAL
RONALD F YALE · THOMAS C SHEPHERD Sr · WILLIAM D SMITH · GREGORY M STONE
ROBERT D WALTERS · ARTHUR WILSON Jr · MICHAEL D WRIGHT · BERNARDO KEALOHA RAMOS
EDWIN G CALHOUN · CHRIS BROWN Jr · MAXIMINO ESTRADA · DOYLE FOSTER
GARY D HALLIDAY · GEORGE THOMPSON Jr · OLIN D MARLAR III · R D McDONELL
ROBERT L WUNDER · RICHARD J ROSSANO · LARRY A SIMONSON · JEROME E JACKSON
DENNIS L WASZKIEWICZ · MANUEL RAMERIZ PUENTES · JACOB B BABIN Jr · ROBERT D COFFEY
JOEL R HANKINS · MARTIN R HUART Jr · WILLIAM A KINDER · VINCE R KISELEWSKI
DAVID RAMIREZ MENDOZA · LAWRENCE PHILLIPS · JAMES M RISCH · GARY A SCHULTZ
ALBERT A VENCEL · OTTO T WIBBEN · GERALD ZLOTORZYNSKI · ROBERT T BRADLEY
ARTHUR L GALLOWAY Jr · WILLIE JOHNSON Jr · THOMAS P OLSON · PAUL E SERVEN
MICHAEL L CROSSLEY · MICHAEL J BAYNE · RONALD J BECKSTED · DONALD C BENNETT
RICHARD J BOEHM · DAVID A BOND · RICHARD R CARSON · CLIFFORD W CORR
WILBERT S DUPREE Jr · JAMES E EDGEMON · KYLE S HAMILTON · DRLEY LEE HATFIELD
MICHAEL S HOLLOWAY · MYRON B JOHNSON · WILLIAM W KIRKPATRICK · RICHARD V KNO
WILLIAM J MILCO · CARL B McGEE · LARRY W McKEE · LAYMON PALMER
TERRY H PRICE · CARL W PRITCHETT · WARREN F RITSEMA · DALLAS D ROBINSON
ROBERT J SCHUMACHER · CLARK V SHAWNEE · JOSEPH R RENK · DONALD M STOTT
RUSSELL L CLAY · WILLIAM G COX · CHARLES H EDWARDS Jr · KENT D ERICKSON
ROBERT M GRIBBLE · TERREL O KIMBER · ROGER A PEDERSON
RICHARD L STANSBARGER · ANDREW R STEWARD Jr · RONALD CLEVELAND
TERRY LEE BOSWORTH · DEWITT W BROWN III · ROBERT J SKEWES
GARY LYNN PACE · THOMAS H RATLIFF · ROBERT LEE
DONALD R BAILEY · RAPHAEL J COLLAZO · ROGER C REID
MICHAEL S McHERN · BILLY RAY PARNELL · MICHAEL L THOMPKINS · ARTHUR HERNANDEZ
CHARLES W STERLING · PHILIP B TERRILL · DONALD J HAVEL · STEVEN C WRAY
JERRY K BOBBITT · JAMES D DAVIS · PETER A WINTER · JAMES E SUTHERLAND
COLLIE JOHNSON Jr · MICHAEL E McPETERS · JAMES R MEADE · WAYNE R BOROWSKI
DOUGLAS E CROOKS · GLENN L HATH · RONALD R BLACKSMITH · ROBERT L KISER
GARY G ZELLER · ARTHUR BEST · RAYFORD H KING · ROBERT TRUJILLO
ALAN D GILBERTSON · FELIX MARCIAL · BENNY E HART
JAMES B LOW · MICHAEL E CIESE · HARLEY W HENDERSON
NOEL B HERNANDEZ
CARLTON J MENDALL
BRUCE C SHOVER
JOHN S WEAVER
DANIEL K ERLANDSON
JAMES M SCHERER
RONNIE BRICE
WILBUR D LATIMER
WILLIAM RUIZ Jr
ROBERT P MARSDEN
ROBERT L HRISOULIS
SAMUEL H BARNETT
KENNETH LOVELACE
WILLIAM H SEABORN Jr
GEORGE R MARR Jr
WILLIAM L MORGAN
GERALD L CARTER
JOHN M NEILL
GARNEY BURLESON Jr
HAROLD B LINEBERGER
JAMES P DUNCAN
PAUL E LEE
LARRY J PEPPER
LOREN D LEBEAU
STEPHEN E WARREN
ROBERT E TAYLOR
PHILIPP R VOLLHARDT
THOMAS A MRAVAC
ROBERT J WILLIAMS
DANIEL J MULLEN
PATRICK J TROTTER
DAVID A SEMMLER
KENNETH W BONESTROO
CARROLL R MILLS
THEODORE R MASON
GARY LEWIS
DOUGLAS R SCHMALTZ
HARRY WOLFENDEN
BARRY L BRINEGAR
ROBERT B GENTRY
JOSEPH W MILEY
JOHNNY MACK TINNEY
DANIEL F FARRELL
JAMES A McINTYRE
BLAKE D WHITNEY
CHRISTOPHER L RAIMEY
RAYMOND F CARROLL
ROBERT A EISENBEISZ
MICHAEL D McGOVERN
DANIEL H TATE
STEVE C ENGLISH

CULTURE

Washington does not belie its role as capital in the field of culture either. The American metropolis boasts many art galleries (especially around Dupont Circle), universities (no less than six, including George Washington University, Georgetown University, the oldest Roman Catholic university in the country and Howard University, the first for black students) some of the most important museums in the world and prestigious foundations such as the Smithsonian Institution and the National Geographic Society. Of course, it is the capital's fulcrum which attracts, in addition to political and historical symbols, the best of the country's nature, art and culture. Around the Mall there are some of the most important museum complexes in the United States: The National Museum of American History, the National Museum of Natural History, the National Gallery of Art, the Smithsonian Institution, which includes the Hirshhorn Museum and Sculpture Garden, the National Air and Space Museum, the Arts and Industries Building, the Arthur M. Sackler Gallery and the Freer Gallery. The collections of a total of fourteen museums and galleries (in addition to the National Zoological Park and the John F. Kennedy Center of the Performing Arts) are run by what is considered to be the largest museum complex in the world and are housed in the confused cluster of buildings, towers and pinnacles known as The Castle. The red-brick building, one of the first examples of American neo-Gothic, was designed in 1855 by J. Renwick. It was a decidedly free composition, as the architect took no account either of the classic layout or the perspective or the stylistic coherence which ought to have reigned in the Mall.
In addition to the museums' administrative offices, The Castle houses the tomb of its founder, the English scientist James Smithson, who died in Genoa, Italy in 1829, leaving $550,000 for the spread of scientific education in the United States, a country he had never visited, but which he admired as an expression of new civil liberties. An act which smacked

106-107 The West Building, with its rotunda at the entrance, houses the old part of the National Gallery of Art's collection, which is one of the world's most important, based on the collection of 125 paintings and 25 sculptures donated in the 1920s by Andrew W. Mellon, Secretary of State at the time. The museum, opened in 1941, is in the Mall and consists of two buildings linked by an underground tunnel. The first Mellon donation was followed by others, from Samuel H. Kress (Italian paintings), Joseph E. Widener (paintings, sculpture and decorative arts) and Chester Dale (French masters). The principal exhibits include Leonardo da Vinci's Portrait of Ginevra de' Benci, Botticelli's Adoration of the Magi and the Portrait of Giuliano de' Medici, Titian's Venus at the Mirror, Monet's Women with Sunshade.

108 top and 109 top The East Building of the National Gallery of Art, designed in 1978 by I.M.Pei, is a modern interpretation of Pope's building. It has a trapezoidal layout consisting of a double triangle with a diagonal gap between the two buildings.

The base of one triangle faces the Capitol and the other one faces Pope's building. The triangular theme is repeated in the glass which covers the building, which is used to house temporary exhibitions and the celebrated modern art collection.

of revenge by a man who, although he was the illegitimate son of an English duke and a descendant of Henry VII, had cruelly suffered from the prevailing climate of respectability in England. Amongst the Smithsonian museums, whose joint collections are estimated to increase by around one million pieces annually, are the Anacostia Museum (African-American history and culture), the National Museum of American Art and the National Portrait Gallery (national portraits and American art, both situated in the Old Patent Office, built in 1836-67 by R. Mills), the Renwick Gallery (American decorative art) and the Arts and Industries Building (American objects from the Victorian period) with its cruciform layout, which was designed in 1888 by Cluss and Schulze. It comes as no surprise to discover that the time required to admire each of the Smithsonian's treasures for one second, working 24 hours a day, is calculated at two and a half years. Not for nothing is it known as the "nation's loft". Dedicated to the history, politics, culture, science and technology of the United States, the National Museum of American History is housed in the building designed in 1964 by McKim, Mead & White. From George Washington's false teeth to the outfit worn by the First Lady during the presidential inauguration ceremony, from the red shoes Judy Garland wore in "The Wizard of Oz" to Muhammed Ali's boxing gloves; weapons, uniforms, medals, coins, textiles, cars, computers provide a 360-degree celebration of the heroic exploits of a Nation. That huge nation whose extraordinary and extremely rich natural heritage is to be found in the National Museum of Natural History, the most visited museum in the world, housed in a building dating from 1910. Amongst its geological, biological and anthropological collections, certain exhibits stand out, such as the Dinosaur Hall, with fossil dinosaur skeletons, the Hall of Gems with precious and semi-precious stones from all over the world, including the Hope Diamond (45 carats) the world's largest blue diamond. Less showy, but equally precious, are the stones exhibited in the Earth, Moon and Metorites Hall, with five moon rocks from the Apollo trips and the world's largest

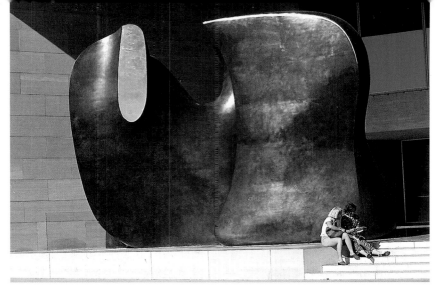

108-109 The National Gallery's West Building was built by John Russell Pope in 1941, to a classical design and was later restored by Keyes Condon Florance. The grandiose building, in pink Tennessee marble, with its monumental staircase, rotunda and cupola inspired by the Pantheon in Rome, was judged by its contemporaries to an antiquated and pompous building.

109 top and bottom The National Gallery owns a rich collection of prints and drawings, made up of more than 50,000 items, including engravings by Rembrandt and Dürer and drawings by Blake.

collection of meteorites. Green Tuscan marble, pink Tennessee marble, travertino from the Roman region of Lazio, Ionic porticos and a marble fountain decorated with a bronze Mercury (attributed to Adriaen de Vries): the credentials of the National Gallery of Art, with its two buildings, are on display right from the very beginning. Inaugurated in 1941 thanks to generous donations from private citizens like Andrew W. Mellon (ex Treasury Secretary, whose idea the museum was), it is considered to be one of the most important art galleries in the world. The West Building, designed by J.E.Pope in the 1920s, fronted by a monumental staircase and two galleries running around the Rotunda in the entrance, has works dating from the 13th to the 19th century, paintings by Giotto, Botticelli, Raphael, Titian, Goya, Manet, Gauguin and Van Gogh. Plus bronzes, tapestries, silver, marble, engravings and drawings. An underground corridor leads to the East Building which has a trapezoid ground plan and was built in 1978 to plans by I.M.Pei. It houses temporary exhibitions and the prestigious modern art collection.
The southern side of the Mall is an irresistible magnet too. This is where the National Air and Space Museum stands, one of the most famous museums in the world (with more than 9 million visitors each year). It was inaugurated in 1976, built to designs by G. Obata. 26 galleries contain the cream of man's challenge to the skies: the Wright brothers' first aeroplane, the 1903 Flyer, the Spirit of St. Louis in which Charles Lindberg crossed the Atlantic non-stop in 1927, the Apollo 11 spacecraft which took Armstrong and his companions to the moon, as well as aeroplanes, missiles, space shuttles, orbital satellites and films on the history of flight. There are five thousand paintings and three thousand sculptures in the collection of the Hirshhorn Museum and Sculpture Garden, housed in the three-floor building designed by G. Bunshaft in 1974. Born out of the modern art collection donated to the American state in 1966 by Joseph H. Hirshhorn, the museum, which is like an enormous ring perched on four great pillars, encloses an entire square. An underground passage leads to the Sculpture Garden,

110 top and 111 top The Smithsonian Institution complex houses the world's greatest museum and consists of several different buildings. The oldest, known as The Castle, was designed in 1849 by James Renwick in neo-Gothic style and houses the administrative departments for the fourteen Smithsonian museums, eight of which are situated in the Mall. The building's site does not fit into Pierre L'Enfant's plan for the Mall either as regards its architecture or its location.

110-111 The Arts&Industries Building, the second oldest building on the Mall, was designed in 1888 by Cluss and Schulze and restored in 1976 by the architect Hugh N. Jacobsen. It has a cruciform ground plan and houses, as well as the exhibits from the Philadelphia Exhibition of 1876, an important collection of Victorian items, including Morse's telegraph. The museum belongs to the prestigious Smithsonian Institution, which was founded thanks to the donation of more than $500,000 bequeathed by an Englishman called James Smithson, the illegitimate son of duke, who wanted in this way to contribute to the development of the sciences in the country of new civil liberties, the United States.

112 bottom and 113 top The National Geographic Society is a non-profit-making scientific institution and is the Smithsonian's equivalent in the field of geography. Its Explorers Hall is dedicated to exploration of the earth and space with video, diorama and computer exhibits. The Society publishes the world-famous magazine National Geographic and is housed in three different buildings along M Street.

112-113 and 112 top The National Museum of Natural History has more visitors than any museum in the world. It is housed in a building which dates from 1910 and has important geology, biology and anthropology collections. Among its 118 exhibits, some of the most important are the Hope Diamond, at 45 carats the world's biggest blue diamond, the fossil skeletons in the Dinosaur Hall and five lunar rocks brought back to earth by the Apollo missions.

which is on a lower level that the Mall, and where sculptures by masters like Rodin, Manzu and Picasso are set amongst fountains and gardens. Underneath the Enid A. Haupt Garden, a Victorian-style public park created in 1987, there are the underground rooms of two museums opened to the public in 1987. These are the Arthur M. Sackler Gallery, dedicated to Asiatic art and the National Museum of African Art, the only institution in the United States dedicated to African Art. The Freer Gallery, inaugurated in 1923 to house the eclectic collection of Asian art belonging to the industrialist Charles Lang Freer, also owns paintings by James McNeill Whistler, a friend of Freer's. There are still other museums in the capital, including the Corcoran Gallery of Art, founded in 1869 with the collection of paintings and sculpture belonging to the banker W.W.Corcoran (to which European works of art were later added), the National Building Museum, dedicated to the American contribution in architecture (and which is characterised by a 96-metre long hall overlooked by all four floors of the building), the Phillips Collection of modern art and Dumbarton Oaks, famous for its collections of Byzantine and pre-Columbian art. There are two museums of Jewish culture: one is the B'nai B'rith Klutznick Museum of the history and art of the Jewish people, including several decorated wedding contracts (ketubahs) dating from the 18th century and originating in Italian towns such as Rome and Ferrara, sacred vestments and liturgical objects. The second one is on Raul Wallenberg Place, on the east side of the Tidal Basin. It is the United States Holocaust Memorial Museum, inaugurated in 1992.

A flag striped in blue, green and brown, symbolising sky, sea and land: this is the emblem of the geographical equivalent of the Smithsonian Institution, the National Geographic Society. Founded in Washington in 1888 by 33 gentlemen, for more than a century now the world's largest non-profit-making scientific and educational association with 11 million members in 170 countries, has been promoting and financing explorations, studying and publicising the assets and the beauties of our planet. From the discovery of the mysterious

114 top and 114-115 The National Museum of American Art, entirely dedicated to painting, sculpture, photography and American ethnic art of the colonial period has been housed since 1968, along with the National Portrait Gallery, in the Old Patent Office Building, which was built by Robert Mills in 1836-67. Amongst its exhibits, the portraits and scenes of Indian life by George Catlin (1796-1872).

Inca city of Machu Picchu to Reinhold Messner's ascent of Everest, the Society offers it readers an exciting world of adventure, discoveries and natural marvels, principally through the legendary yellow National Geographic magazine (read by more than 40 million people with more than 10 million subscribers). The prestigious foundation occupies three buildings: the Hubbard Memorial Hall (1903), the stepped structure similar to a Mayan pyramid built by Skidmore, Owings and Merril in 1984 and the marble and glass building put up in 1964 by E.D. Stone.

They contain Explorers Hall, with computers and dioramas with which to find out about the earth and space, an amphitheatre for interactive programmes and a gigantic globe, three metres high with a circumference of ten.

But Washington's hunger for culture does not stop here. Although up until the middle of the Sixties, as Mel Elfin, the director of the US News and World Report wrote in 1988, Washington had a symphony orchestra which played in a hall whose acoustics rivalled a railway tunnel underneath the Swiss Alps, it now has not one but several auditoria of international standard. The first of these is the John F. Kennedy Center for the Performing Arts, at Foggy Bottom. The complex, built thanks to donations from 60 countries (Italy, for example, supplied the Carrara marble used for the cladding) stretches along the Potomac and includes halls for concerts, ballets and stage productions as well as the American Film Institute. There is the national Symphony Orchestra Concert Hall and a gigantic concert hall which holds 22,000 people. On Capitol Hill there is the Folger Shakespeare Library, built in the classic style in the 1930s, with a replica of an Elizabethan theatre and a precious collection of rare editions; south of the Capitol lie the buildings housing the Library of Congress (18 million volumes!): the Thomas Jefferson Building, which houses the donation of the third president's personal library, the John Adams Building and the James Madison Building, with manuscripts, a newspaper and periodicals library, maps and rare books, such as the 1455 Gutenberg Bible.

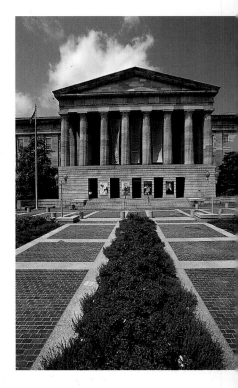

115 The National Portrait Gallery, on the south side of the Old Patent Office Building, houses the portraits of the most nation's illustrious people, including all the presidents. These include a bust of George Washington by Houdon, a gesso by Paul Troubetzkoy of Franklin D. Roosevelt and a portrait of Richard Nixon by Norman Rockwell. The ground floor is entirely dedicated to exhibits from the Meserve photograph collection.

116-117 The National Portrait Gallery's Great Hall, sumptuously decorated with stucco and windows in American Victorian Renaissance style, is one of the largest of the Old Patent Office's exhibition spaces. The building, which as its name suggests, was used for 92 years as the offices of the American patents office, is located between G Street and F Street.

117

118 top, centre and bottom The National Air and Space Museum, located on the south side of the Mall, is the most popular of all the museums the Smithsonian administers. With more than 9 million visitors, the collection is housed in a 1976 building designed by Gyo Obata and includes hundreds of aircraft, space capsules and missiles, including the Apollo 11 which took Armstrong and companions to the moon and the Gemini 4 spacecraft from which the first spacewalk was made in 1965.

118-119 and 119 top In the National Air and Space Museum's 26 galleries, visitors can see the very best of the history of flight, from the first air balloons to the most recent space capsules, including a collection dedicated to the history of astronomy, from ancient times right up to our own days. The museum also includes the Samuel P. Langley Theater, which shows films on the history of flight and space, filmed in IMAX high-yield photography films.

120-121 The Hirshhorn Museum, built in 1974, faces onto a circular courtyard, decorated in the centre with a fountain. The museum, which houses almost five thousand modern and contemporary paintings and sculptures, was founded in 1966 with the donation from the businessman Joseph H. Hirshhorn, son of poverty-stricken Lithuanians who emigrated to the United States when the future financier was just six. The collection includes works by Degas, Matisse, Medardo Rosso, Picasso, Morandi and Gauguin.

121 top, center and bottom Compared to a bunker, because of its massive three-storey circular structure, resting on massive pillars, relieved only by a narrow window and balcony, the Hirshhorn Museum boasts one of the Mall's most exciting places, the Sculpture Garden, which has in it pieces of modern sculpture such as the Horse and Rider by Marino Marini (1952-53) and the Seated Woman by Henry Moore (1956-57) shown in the photograph. There are also pieces by Rodin, Brancusi, Calder and Fontana.

124-125 The Great Hall of the National Building Museum is indeed great. It is in fact 96 metres long by 35 metres wide and 48 metres high. Four floors with arches and balconies face onto its interior, with eight 23-metre high Corinthian columns which are 7.5 metres in diameter. It was here that the Inauguration Balls of Presidents Nixon, Carter, Reagan and Bush were held.

126-167 Each year 18 million visitors come to Washington and it is the most scenically grandiose of all United States cities. Seen also as the country's richest as regards museums, monuments, art galleries, scientific and cultural institutions, this Virginian city is, first and foremost, a symbol of a great country.

122-123 top The Holocaust Memorial Museum, built on the east side of the Tidal Basin, is dedicated to the millions of Jews and the other victims of nazism - homosexuals, communists, Romanies, handicapped people, political prisoners - who died during World War II. The building, by James Ingo Freed, includes documents, photographs, newspaper cuttings and objects from the concentration camps.

122-123 The National Building Museum is housed in the Pension Building, built in 1882-87 for war pensions business, which remained there until 1926. Built in Renaissance style, it was restored in 1980 and five years later housed exhibitions on the history of American architecture.

128 The statue of Abraham Lincoln, encircled by a classical colonnade built in 1922, is a monument to the man who, as the first president of the United States, is considered by the Americans as one time "father" of the country.

WASHINGTON

ILLUSTRATION CREDITS

All the photographs are by Massimo Borchi except the following:

Grant Faint / The Image Bank: page 1

The Image Bank: pages 126-127

Photobank: pages 12, 32 top, 48, 49, 96-97

Andrea Pistolesi: pages 2-3, 16, 20-21, 24 top, 27 top, 34-35, 36, 37, 38 top, 38-39, 40 left, 40-41, 46, 46-47, 50-51, 69, 87, 100 top, 102-103, 104-105, 122-123, 123 top, 128.

Guido Alberto Rossi / The Image Bank: pages 84-85, 90-91, 93

Galen Rowell / Ag. Franca Speranza: pages 6-7

Pamela J. Zilly / The Image Bank: page 13